WORLD
MOTORCYCLE
ENDURANCE RACING

WORLD MOTORCYCLE ENDURANCE RACING

Mark Wernham and
Mick Walker

OSPREY
AUTOMOTIVE

First published in Great Britain in 1994
by Osprey, an imprint of Reed Consumer
Books Limited, Michelin House,
81 Fulham Road, London SW3 6RB and
Auckland, Melbourne, Singapore and Toronto.

ISBN 1 85532 434 2

Project Editor Shaun Barrington
Editor Simon McAuslane
Page design Paul Kime/Ward Peacock
Partnership

Printed and bound in Hong Kong
Produced by Mandarin Offset

Front cover
*Kawasaki France, Bontempi, Le Mans
1993*

Back cover
*The evening descends upon the pitlanes,
Spa, Belgium*

Half-title page
*Superb view of the Frenchman
Monneret's Finacor Yamaha, Bol d'Or
1993*

Title page
*Refuelling is an important part of the
pit crew's duties*

Right
*Ducati rider Pascal Picotte rushes out
of the pits at the 1993 Bol d'Or*

**Photographs by Mark Wernham,
with grateful thanks to Kel Edge
for additional historical images,
and to Mick Walker.**

For a catalogue of all books published by Osprey Automotive
please write to:

**The Marketing Department, Reed Consumer Books,
1st Floor, Michelin House, 81 Fulham Road, London SW3 6RB**

Contents

Imagine hard charging like this for twenty-four hours! Privateer Daffix Eurocol Honda, Le Mans April 1993

Early Days

The honour of being the first country to organise and promote road racing and to encourage truly long-distance events must go to France.

Well before the end of the nineteenth century, several separate French-based individuals had created organisations to explore the use of the yet untried Otto-cycle engine and thus create a fledgling motorcycle industry.

These early pioneers included men such as: Count de Dion and his mechanic Georges Bouton; Maurice Fournier, Felix Theodore Millet and Ernest Michaux. In addition, the Russian-born brothers Eugene and Michel Werner had settled in France and become Frenchmen through adoption. All these men had a hand in placing France at the very vanguard of motorcycle innovation as the twentieth century began.

Much of the original technical development concerning automobile, aviation and motorcycling interests was carried out by the French. But strangely, although they built up a considerable automobile and aviation presence in world markets in the following decades, French motorcycling didn't benefit in the same way. In fact only Peugeot and Motobecane were destined to grow into large concerns, and they both largely restricted their efforts to the domestic market.

The first recorded endurance race was the Paris to Dieppe event of 1897. Early feats of endurance were usually staged over public roads, and as time went by these point to point races became longer. For example, the Paris-Prague of 1907 came about largely as a result of the Czech cyclist, Vaclav Klement (who founded the Laurin & Klement factory in 1895 – at first making bicycles and later motorcycles) visiting Paris.

Czechoslovakia, like France, was one of the early leaders in motorcycle sport and in 1905 Vaclav Vondrich won the prestigious Coupe Internationale des Motocyclettes, at Dowden in France, considered to be the official world championship.

As a further example it is worth noting that with a production of over 3000 motorcycles in 1907, Laurin and Klement was one of Europe's leading factories of the period.

Meanwhile in Britain, racing suffered thanks to a blanket 20 mph speed limit enforced everywhere within the United Kingdom with the exception of the Isle of Man.

The start of the 1993 Le Mans 24 Hours. Note the superb facilities – a far cry from endurance racing in bygone days

Above

A rider awaits his turn out on the circuit; endurance racing calls for not only skill, but patience too

Left

Another 1993 Le Mans shot; the works Suzuki GSXR of Graziano just before a con-rod let go, forcing the bike into an early retirement

The Isle of Man, with its own parliament, could not only close its roads but its authorities were by then accustomed to collaborating in competition and welcomed racers. The famous TT (Tourist Trophy) began in 1907, which in many ways was a feat of endurance, although the 'tourist' part soon went by the board.

In America, long-distance racing also found an enthusiastic following in these early days, and like France, the USA can be regarded as one of the true pioneers in the development of the motorcycle – both for street and competition use. During the first decade of the twentieth century the American industry grew at a tremendous rate, with the likes of Excelsior, Harley-Davidson, Indian and Flying Merkel leading the way.

From a racing standpoint, the first of the Stateside manufacturers to enter the ring were Indian and Curtiss. The former concern was the result of two racing cyclists, George M Hendee and Carl Oscar Hedstrom pooling their resources in 1901 to form the Indian marque.

Above
Swiss Bolliger Kawasaki rider. Hardly dressed for fashion, rather to keep the elements at bay including oversuit to keep rider dry and warm. Note duct-tape to prevent visor from steaming up

Left
Conditions are not always favourable on the track as this shot from the 1990 Le Mans 24 Hours proves

Efficient (and quick!) pit-stops are all-important. Endurance racing is all about track-time – not wasting it in the pits

When a bike pits, the mechanics must be able to pin point the problems quickly

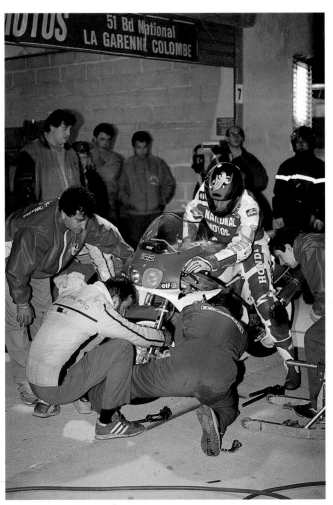

Wilfred Veille keeping up the pace as the sun goes down during the 1993 Le Mans marathon. He was drafted into the factory Kawasaki squad to replace Terry Rymer after the Englishman had crashed during qualifying

The first Indian motorcycles to take part in a competition event appeared in July 1902 when three examples were entered in the Boston-New York endurance run – the first such event ever staged in North America. In true pioneering fashion Hendee and Hedstrom acted as riders, together with George N Holden. The trio scored a resounding 1, 2, 3 to firmly establish the Indian name in the record books. In September 1903 Indian rider Holden won the country's first long-distance track race at the Brighton Beach dirt track, New York City.

An interesting feature of these early Indian machines was the 'bought in' single cylinder engine produced for them by the Thor Manufacturing Co. Another point of interest was the chain final drive, when most of the competition were still using belts.

The first of the famous v-twins did not appear until 1925. George Holden again grabbed the headlines when he and Louis Mueller

established a new coast-to-coast record of 31 days, 12 hours and 15 minutes.

The Indian v-twin first appeared in 1907 and that year an example was sent to Britain, where the American rider T.K. Hastings rode it in the Thousand Mile Trial organised by the ACC (Auto Cycle Club)' – itself a forerunner of the ACU (Auto Cycle Union). This event was later to evolve into the legendary ISDT (International Six Days Trial). It was the first time that an American machine ridden by an American had won a British motorcycle event.

By 1908 speed contests were quickly taking the place of endurance runs, the precursors of true endurance racing.

'Swede' Swenson won the 978 mile New York-Chicago race that year while in Britain T.K. Hastings repeated his victory of 12 months earlier winning the 1908 Thousand Mile Trial.

Above

Not quite how to do it... the endurance racer's nightmare is a crash in which the the bike is damaged to such an extent it can't continue. This one actually finished!

Right

One of the works Kawasakis taking on extra lubricant. It is vitally important that the oil level does not fall during a long distance race

A Curtiss first came to notice in 1902 when an example set up the fastest time for a 'standard machine' in the New York Motorcycle Club's road race. The man behind the name was Glenn H Curtiss, who today is far better known for his aviation, rather than motorcycling expertise. But in those far off days Curtiss was to play a vital role in the birth of the racing motorcycle in the USA.

Most of this great pioneer's exploits are outside the scope of this book, but it is worth noting that he set up a large number of records, many of which were to remain undefeated for a number of years. He was also a brilliant designer and in early 1904 a Curtiss twin became the first motorcycle in history with twist-grip controls.

During 1910, Oscar Hedstrom had begun mapping out new four and eight valve singles and v-twins and, from the middle of 1911, these appeared and were to form the mainspring of Indian's racing and record-breaking activities until the mid 1920s. It is interesting to realise that the four-valve per cylinder layout was not intended as a means of extra power, but to improve reliability; it was nonetheless a noteworthy technical achievement.

1911 saw the first 'foreign' victory in the Isle of Man TT series – gained by Indian's number 1 rider, Jake De Rosier. Also in 1911, another Indian rider, C.B. Franklin, rode one of the new eight valve twins at the Brooklands circuit to cover 300 miles in less than 300 minutes, establishing official world speed records for the 2, 4, 5 and 6 hour periods.

Back in America board tracks (otherwise known as motordromes) had arrived in 1908 and quickly spread to dominate motorcycle sport across the states for the next few years. This, combined with hill climbing, dirt track and speedway, was very much the American path for bike sport for much of the 1920s and 1930s.

Even so, there was still the odd long distance event including even 24 hour races. The sheer size of North America lent itself to epic record-breaking runs such as the 1,685 mile Three Flags classic from Canada to Mexico. Other well-known marathons included the 1244 miles of mainly dirt roads from Denver to Chicago and, of course, the epic coast-to-coast journey.

But what was to become the most famous long-distance race of all was launched in France, in 1922. With a total of 28 entries in its first year, the Bol d'Or race was to grow into one of France's most prestigious sporting events.

As detailed elsewhere, the first Bol d'Or was held at Vaujours and the winner was Zind (riding a 500 Motosacoche). Endurance racing as we

Night-time action, with the track and pits a blaze of light. This is Le Mans in 1993

it today can trace its true origins back to the inaugural Bol d'Or. Earlier events were more for specialised racing machinery, or simply a form of long-distance trial, rather than a real race. In addition, most events prior to the outbreak of the Great War in 1914 were held over dirt, rather than tarmac roads.

Development of endurance racers has always tended to go hand-in-hand with street-going machines and the general basics of motorcycling. Over the years roadsters have ultimately benefited from endurance racing, as new developments take place first on the track before the next generation of products appear in the showroom. As roadsters improve, the endurance racers are provided with better performance, handling, braking and reliability to withstand the rigours of 24 hours of non-stop abuse.

As well as prototypes eventually being put into production, details such as tyres, suspension, brakes, chains and even electrical components have all been improved over the years.

The endurance racing machine has actually been responsible for many advances in ordinary motorcycles – the fact is that full Grand Prix bikes get the attention of the press, while endurance bikes do much of the real testing for the machines sold to the public.

In this, the endurance racing circus, are the real unsung heroes of motorcycle sport. Over the next chapters we'll look at the events, the engineers and the riders who have shaped two-wheel history.

Above
In the Superbike category of the 1993 Le Mans 24 Hours, the Suzuki of Daridan, Danzer and Remaud races through the night to a fifth in class, 22nd overall

Right
The smiles of victory. Left to right: National Motos, Kawasaki France and Daffix Eurocol teams after the 1993 Le Mans 24 Hours

The Bol d'Or

One can trace the Bol d'Or 24 hour race right back to 1922, and this French classic is easily the longest running day and night event in the motorcycle racing calendar. In fact it would be true to say that it dominates the endurance racing scene, carrying with it the biggest prestige and the richest prizes, almost equalling a full Grand Prix world championship meeting.

The very first Bol d'Or saw the two-wheelers racing non-stop for some 48 (yes forty eight!) hours. This was followed by a similar event for cyclecars and sidecars; this extravaganza ran from 27-29 May 1922 and in the motorcycle solo event there were separate categories for 250, 350 and 500cc machines.

As this event was staged some 12 months before the first 24 hour car race at Le Mans, it was bikes which sparked the French passion for long distance racing.

This first Bol d'Or was held at the Vaujours circuit and was won by a 500cc Motosacohe which covered 1,245 kilometres (774 miles) in the 24 hour period. From 1923 through to 1936 the race was held at St. Germain, except for 1927 when Fontainebleau was the venue. Then in 1937, the Bol d'Or moved to the legendary Montlhéry circuit. During the Inter-war period, besides the original Motosacoche success, victory was secured by: Sunbeam (3), FN (1), Gillet-Herstal (3), Monet-Goyon (1), Velocette (3), Jonghi (1), Norton (2), Harley Davidson (1), Motobécane (1) and another by Motosacoche.

The Bol d'Or was reinstated after the war at St. Germain in 1947, where it was won by Gustave Lefevre on a plunger-framed 500 International Norton. Lefevre went on to record another six victories, the last one in 1957, making him the most successful rider in Bol d'Or history.

Back in 1950, the first scooter had entered the event and throughout the decade these small wheel machines took part in considerable numbers. The most impressive being the Italian Rumi marque. As the 1960s dawned a general depression hit the motorcycle (and scooter) business, and their were only 31 starters for the 1960 Bol d'Or from which only 10 teams were still in circulation at the end of 24 hours. This lack of entries

The first ever Bol d'Or took place in 1922 and has since risen to become the world's premier endurance race. This photograph dates from 1983 and was taken at sunrise on the Mistral Straight

was unfortunately mirrored in a depressingly meagre number of spectators with only 800 turning up. The resulting financial loss meant that there was no Bol d'Or race from 1961 to 1968.

What saved the event – and most probably endurance racing in general – was the advent of the modern Superbike in the shape of Honda's magnificent four pot CB750.

Montlhéry was again the stage for the re-launch of the famous French marathon and the 1969 race saw several factory-backed entries, including the Honda ridden by the pairing of Rougerie and Urdich and entered through the Parisian dealers Japauto.

Works Triumph Tridents contested the 1970 event and duly took the chequered flag, piloted by Britons Paul Smart and Tom Dickie.

Factory participation in events such as Daytona and the Imola 200 meant that, before long, race kits became available to private teams (provided of course that you were well-heeled, as the kits often exceeded

Above

Another famous name associated with the Bol d'Or is the Swiss frame constructor Fritz Egli. This 1100cc Egli Kawasaki is a 1981 machine

left

The Parisian Japauto concern gained worldwide fame when its Honda engined bikes won the Bol d'Or in 1972 and 1973. A 1062cc Japauto-Honda as raced in the 1981 event by Bolle and Bertin

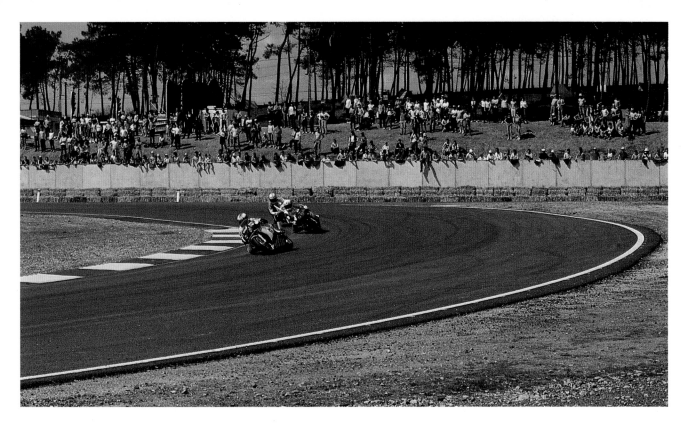

Above left

Besides the racing there are many other facets of the Bol d'Or and of other events, including showmen like this wheelie exponent at Le Mans

Left

The leading works Honda RVF during the 1987 race; Honda found the opposition much tougher than it had in its domineering days of the previous decade

Above

Endurance racing has always found an enthusiastic audience in France, not only for the Bol d'Or at the Paul Ricard circuit, but also for the Le Mans race

Overleaf

Monneret's Finacor Yamaha ran well in the 1993 Bol d'Or until the seventeenth hour, when it retired

the initial bike price!). European factories such as Moto Guzzi, BMW, Laverda and Ducati soon got into the act too, largely taking their place following the failure of the British motorcycle industry in the early 1970s. Soon the Bol d'Or and the other endurance races became an intercontinental battlefield, a contest between Europe and Japan.

The Montlhéry circuit could no longer accommodate the growing importance and (sheer size!) of the race and was moved in 1971 to the Bugatti circuit at Le Mans. This move was to be a wise one and largely instrumental in the Bol d'Or's rise to pre-eminence amongst today's endurance races.

Le Mans, due to the shape of the town and circuit, was an ideal setting. Added to this is the atmosphere built up in the days preceding the annual event – racing only forming a part of what is virtually a week-long carnival. The circuit itself features a wide array of amenities with everything from a comprehensive camp site, through bike shows to discos. The organisers cleverly combine the thrill of racing with an unmatched array of other attractions in a way no-one else has achieved, even at Grand Prix level.

Although another British victory was achieved in 1971 – Pickrell/Tait on a BSA Rocket Three – the 1970s were largely the era of Japanese four-cylinder machines from Honda and Kawasaki at the Bol d'Or.

The first of two victories for Japauto-entered Hondas came in 1972, when Debrock and Ruiz won on a 969cc Japauto housed in a Dresda chassis and weighing in at only 170 kg (375 lb). This year also saw the

Godier and Genoud pairing appear for the first time; they finished runners-up riding a 750 Honda housed in a Swiss Egli chassis.

Fritz Egli, in typical fashion, created some interesting features in its design. These included an 8-litre oil tank to avoid using an oil-cooler and also doing away with the need to top up the oil during pit calls. Cast alloy wheels, a four-into-one exhaust system and effective streamlining were all items which other teams would copy in future years.

Less than half the teams finished and in many ways 1972 was to be the last year of the true amateur in this event. 1973 saw the arrival of a mass of official factor-interest and purpose-built bikes on a much wider scale. At the same time capacity classes were scrapped; what mattered now was outright victory.

The year also marked the début in the Bol d'Or of Kawasaki's new 903cc ZI, ten of which were entered, including official machines from the

Above
The pair of Kawasaki France factory ZXR750s which posed such a threat in the 1993 championship series, but failed to deliver the goods at the final hurdle

Right
Graziano and his team led the 1993 Bol d'Or until 9pm when he collided with Simon Buckmaster of Phase One. Graziano pushed his Suzuki back to the pits after the crash, losing one hour in total. The machine was repaired and re-entered the race, finally finishing an incredible fifth, only fifteen laps behind the winners

French importer SIDEMM. These came complete with factory mechanics and 'Pops' Yoshimura Junior.

Against these were lined many interesting bikes ranging from the new Yamaha XS750 triple, TZ350, a pair of Suzuki 750 Daytona triples, John Player Nortons, works BMWs, Laverdas, Moto Guzzis and no less than fourteen Hondas; in the shape of the race winning 969cc Japauto (for the second year running), an 820, an 810, eight 750s (three of which were works entries) and three of the new CB 500 four cylinder models.

BMW had made an official return to solo racing with their new R90S motors equipped with 38mm Dell'Orlo cabs and producing a claimed 84bhp. The engines were 'lifted' to provide additional ground clearance and careful pruning had reduced dry weight from 218kg (481 lb) down to 180kg (397 lb). All this paid off with the leading German twin coming home a respectable third.

Although Japauto (Honda) and BMW had shared two of the top three placings, it is worth noting that all the others on the leaderboard were

Above
Time-keepers and signallers keep in touch with the bikes through the hours of darkness. Without these team members there would be no endurance racing

Left
The unlucky Simon Buckmaster on the British Phase One Kawasaki ZXR750 before the infamous accident which ended his racing career

Kawasakis. If this had been forgotten by the time the next Bol d'Or came around, everyone was to receive a reminder.

1974 was to be the year of Godier, Genoud and Big K. Replacing their Honda engine with a ZI in another Egli chassis they not only completed a longer distance than anyone had done before in Bol d'Or history, but also chalked up wins in the Barcelona 24 hours, the 1000 Kms at Mettet in Belgium and were runners-up at the Spa 24 hour race. All this success ensured that they were crowned FIM Coupe d'Endurance champions.

More success came in 1975 for Godier/Genoud and Kawasaki with another win at the Bol d'Or, this time with the engine capacity upped to 1100cc. The Kawasaki factory also played its role, having the most comprehensive team back-up ever seen in endurance racing. This was to pay golden dividends, with the marque taking the top three places that year.

The following year, 1976, saw Honda respond with a serious attack on

Above
English rider Terry Rymer was the 1992 World Endurance Champion. Kawasaki France brought him into their squad for the 1993 Bol d'Or, but engine problems thwarted success

Left
Privateer team Daffix Eurocol hit problems and retired after eight hours, dropping them from the 1993 title chase

the Coupe d'Endurance championship – the beginning of the factory dominance in endurance racing which is described later in this book. What should be recognised is the important part that the Bol d'Or played in reaching this peak of development.

Above

The 1992 World Superbike Champion Doug Polen used all his skills on a Ducati to race to second place in the first two hours of the 1993 Bol d'Or before problems struck. Although they fought back to sixth place, they were soon out of the reckoning and retired at three-quarter race distance

Right

Crowd invasion before the end of the scheduled 24 hours is a normal feature of the great French endurance classic. This shot is from the 1987 event

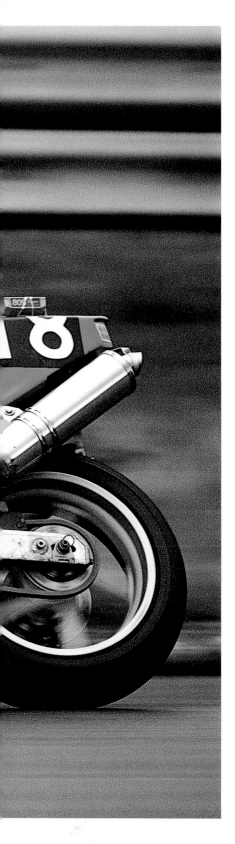

Thruxton 500 miler

Thruxton airfield in Hampshire was the scene of countless endurance racing battles during much of the 1950s and 1960s. These continued in the the 1970s, albeit in a shortened form (400 miles) during its final years.

   The inaugural event was staged one fine summer's day in June 1955 over a 2.76 mile circuit arranged at the airfield venue. The rules for this first event stated that two riders would be allowed for each machine and the winning team was to be the pairing which had piled up the most laps by the ninth hour.

Below

How it used to be; Brian Setchell on the Syd Lawton Norton 650SS which he shared with Phil Read to win the 1962 Thruxton 500 mile race

Left

The nearest thing to the Setchell/Read Norton today an 888 Ducati V-twin. This one was raced by Swedish riders Larson and Jonsson at Anderstorp, 18-20 June 1993; and finished nineteenth

The original concept was to run either a 12 or 24 hour race, part of which would be in darkness. However, it was eventually decided that for this first event, at any rate, nine hours would suffice.

As things turned out, for the majority of the competitors nine hours was quite long enough. Surprisingly, the real problem which surfaced was tyre – not rider fatigue or mechanical retirement. This was due to the abrasive nature of the Thruxton tarmac. Front tyres seemed to suffer more than rear ones. This was to cause near panic, as very few teams had come prepared with spare rubber, let alone spare wheels and tyres. Countless SOS calls were relayed over the public address system. As a result, many spectators provided tyres from their own bikes, whilst mechanics were despatched to the local town of Andover in a desperate search.

The winners of this first Thruxton marathon were Eddie Crooks and Eddie Dow on a 500 BSA Gold Star single. The considerable publicity generated by the original event ensured a much higher standard of entry the following year, with several top riders among the 60 teams.

Even though there was a host of large capacity machines from the likes of Triumph, BSA, Royal Enfield, Norton and Velocette, it was a 350, a Gold Star, which won.

If anyone had placed bets that a Gold Star couldn't win a third time around they would have lost. Rex Avery and partner Fred Webber took their Gold Star to victory in 1957, making it three wins in a row for the BSA single.

An interesting aside was that the Avery/Webber bike finished the 1956 event third overall and had since then covered 12,000 road miles, with only new valves and springs fitted during the entire period.

In 1958, the event became the Thruxton 500 Mile Race, and with it came new levels of interest from manufacturers, press and public alike. Not only this, but for the first time a multi-cylinder machine took the chequered flag, in the shape of a Triumph Tiger 110 ridden by Dan Shorey and future legend Mike Hailwood. The pair completed 220 laps in a time of 7 hours, 35 minutes at an average speed of 66 mph. For the first time none of the top six finishers overall was mounted on a Gold Star and all were twins: Triumph first and fifth, Royal Enfield second and third, Norton sixth; whilst the first ever foreign entry, a 600 BMW R69, came home fourth.

The 1959 '500 miler' saw a BMW take victory. Early leaders Bob McIntyre and Eric Hinton's bid came to an end after the primary chain case shed its lubricant and the chain broke. After repairs, McIntyre's subsequent fall at the Anchor Corner chicane brought dreams of victory to

Not all endurance races are staged in ideal conditions, as witnessed at the start of the 1993 Anderstorp 24 hour race

Above

Although all qualifying and race days were wet, competitors also had their fair share of nice weather, as this scene from Anderstorp, 1993, shows

Left

Swedish heroes Bosson, Linden and Skold used local track knowledge to bring them home second in the 1993 Anderstorp marathon

an end. The lead then transferred to a Triumph Bonneville (new that year) of Godfrey and Holder, but a seven minute pit stop at the half-way stage to fix a loose dynamo ultimately cost them the race.

BSA Gold Stars won both the 1000cc single cylinder and 350cc categories, whilst an NSU Max made it two German wins by taking the freshly introduced 250cc class. *The Motor Cycle* reported: 'This year's 500 miler was the best in the series and was attended by a record crowd and held in brilliant weather.'

As the new decade dawned, the Thruxton 500 Mile Race was more closely disputed than ever, with an ever growing number of factory bikes thinly disguised as dealer entries. The performances of these machines (although clearly non-standard!) were highly publicized by the press and in the sales brochures of the respective manufacturers. A win at Thruxton was held in high esteem and was a major weapon with which to attack

Above
American Doug Toland proved in 1993 that it was still possible to become Endurance Racing World Champion as a privateer. He is seen here at the Anderstorp round on the Phase One Kawasaki

Left
Scotsman Brian Morrison displayed all his skills in the wet conditions at Anderstorp in 1993 to take the works Kawasaki ZXR750 to a second consecutive win and maintain his lead in the championship

rivals on the showroom floor.

1961 was the first year that two long-distance races had been staged in Britain since the war. The Thruxton marathon was joined by an event at Silverstone, organised by BMCRC (British Motor Cycle Racing Club) called the 1000 kilometres. This latter event lasted two more years, before Thruxton reverted to its solus role as the British long distance race for standard production motorcycles.

Another first was chalked up the same year when a Japanese Honda took the Thruxton lightweight (250cc) honours. But at least British bike buffs could take heart from the fact that overall victory went to a Triumph Bonneville ridden by Tony Godfrey and John Holder.

Stars abounded that year, even if they didn't do the winning, with names such as: Bob McIntyre, Alastair King, John Hartle, Phil Read, Sammy Miller, Cecil Sandford and former World Speedway Champion Tommy Price competing.

The beginning of a famous combination, Phil Read and Brian Setchell on Syd Lawton's Norton 650SS, was the star of the 1962 Thruxton marathon. Quite simply, it just cleared off at the start and won by a cool seven laps over its nearest challenger. The same year also witnessed a rapidly deteriorating track surface, which had begun to crack up badly. One must remember that Thruxton was still only an old wartime airfield with straw bales to mark out the course – not a purpose built circuit as it is today.

Read and Setchell made it a double the following year, and on the same bike too, and if this was not enough the partnership of riders and machine won yet again. This was the tenth Thruxton endurance race and it also happened to be the last for a number of years.

The following year, 1965, saw the (now famous) event moved to Castle Combe in Wiltshire. This was necessary because the years of racing, combined with neglect, had wreaked havoc on the Thruxton tarmac surface. The 500-miler did not return to its original home for several years, being staged first at Castle Combe and then at Brands Hatch.

A return was made in 1969, when a new 2.356 mile circuit was opened for bikes. The revised layout bypassed the old finishing straight and the new 'straight' was so short that riders had little time to relax. A flat out, left-right sweep beyond the starting area was entirely new. Even where part of the old course came into play, the series of first bends kept men and machines working hard. Slowing from the 120mph-plus uphill dash to the new, tight, Club Hairpin, exhausted brakes – and nerves – for machines were cranked over while braking.

Peter Linden is a pilot in the Royal Swedish Air Force. His squadron mates treated the pit lane and crowd to a few aerial antics

In the actual race, drama of a different kind made the headlines. While Percy Tait and Malcolm Uphill roared to a record-breaking victory on their factory-supported Triumph Bonneville at an average speed of 84.3 mph near disaster loomed for several other riders as a marshal dashed into the track just yards ahead of them. Anxious to remove a numberplate fallen from a bike, he had completely misjudged the speed of the approach pack of machines. *Motor Cycle* called it 'A miracle escape.'

In 1970, the FIM allowed prototypes to compete in both the Bol d'Or and the Thruxton 500-miler. Norton's new Norvil Commando, ridden by Peter Williams and Charlie Sanby, won after one of the worst rainstorms of any endurance event arrived as the riders completed the first hour lasting for the remainder of the day. As someone who took part in this race, I can recall it all too well.

From the early 1970s the British round of what was now the World

Above
After the brand new pits at Le Mans, the Anderstorp facilities were slightly more basic

Right
Phase One team rider Simon Buckmaster in the cold light of an Anderstorp dawn

Endurance Series struggled to attract spectators. Several attempts were made to broaden its appeal without much success, including a move to Brands Hatch. In 1975 it was shortened to a 400 mile race and, later still, to a 1000 kilometre event. There was even one attempt, at Thruxton, to liven up the proceedings by running a shorter, F750 race among the endurance racers, but this only caused more confusion.

Left
Works Suzuki GSXR rider Graziano awaits team-mate Simeon at Spa

Right
Graziano showing signs of pressure. Endurance racing is all about concentration, skill and determination – all three of these are shown on the rider's face

Above
This CBR600 Honda of Sunby, Borch and Sorensen from the Netherlands came home a very creditable seventeenth overall at Anderstorp

Above
After Anderstorp, Kawasaki France riders Morrison (right) and Veille (left) had two wins each and comfortably led the championship standings

Right
The locals were absolutely delighted with the runner-up spot gained by Bosson, Linden and Skold, and after a little encouragement, celebrated in style

Barcelona 24 Horas

Montjuich Park, Barcelona, was without doubt the most difficult and destructive race of the endurance series. This is true not only because of the difficulties inherent in the famous 2.73 mile lap – consisting of a great number of sharp bends and quick descents of Montjuich – but also because of the extreme demands on both riders and the mechanical components of the machines themselves.

The event was inaugurated in 1955 by the Pena Motorista Barcelona and was held without interruption until a series of accidents brought its

One of the greatest wins in the history of the Barcelona 24 Horas came in 1967 when the Ossa factory won at record speed with a 230cc single ridden by Carlos Giro and Luis Yglesias

Although the famous Montjuich Park, Barcelona marathon is no longer held, the same cannot be said of the Spa 24 hour race. The grid at the 1993 event reflected not just this individual race, but the championship overall

curtailment some three decades later. During this time it became, with the Bol d'Or, the most famous endurance race in the world.

Initially the event was solely intended to be a feat of endurance in which the simple act of finishing was, in itself, a test of the powers of both rider and machine. However, it was to develop over the years into a genuine road race; a test of both endurance and speed in which victory brought tremendous prestige, not only in Spain but all around the world.

Victory in the first Barcelona 24 Horas (Hours) went to a 125cc Montesa which completed 510 laps of the arduous course. Montesa also took victory in 1956. From this humble start was to come an ever increasing number of entries and international recognition. The first non-Spanish victory went to the Italian Ducati marque.

Ducati's Montjuich debut came in July 1957, and helped to establish its new offshoot in Spain, the Barcelona-based Mototrans factory. Paired with

their ace rider Bruno Spaggiari was a newcomer to the Ducati team, Alberto Gandossi. The machine they used was a 125cc version of the factory's 100 Gram Sport. This had originally been prepared back in Bologna for the Milano-Taranto road event, now cancelled following the earlier Mille Miglia disaster in which several spectators had been killed when a competitor's car left the road.

The team of Spaggiari/Gandossi covered a total of 586 laps to win the event outright after 24 hours, at an average speed of 57.66mph, covering 1,385 miles in the process. Ducatis filled the next couple of places and this was to be the start of a continued Ducati presence over the next quarter of a century, in which they were to be the most successful marque in the 24 Horas history.

Ducati were fully committed to their Grand Prix efforts in 1958 and 1959, but returned in 1960 when no less than eight 175 models contested

Kawasaki France rider Brian Morrison did not seem to need inspiration; things were later to change on the Belgian circuit

The Daffix-Eurocel Honda, with team umbrella and supporter, awaits the action at Spa

the Barcelona marathon with a variety of Spanish and Italian riders. Franceso Villa and Amedco Balboni won, averaging 59.25mph, with 603 laps completed. This Ducati win was against formidable opposition, which included the likes of the British pairing of Peter Darville and Bruce Daniels on an MLG-entered 600cc BMW R69S.

The tables were turned the following year when Darville, this time partnered by Norman Price, completed a record 613 laps in the 24 hour period.

The Le Mans-type start is always an exciting feature of endurance racing. This one shows things getting under way as riders sprint to their machinery at Spa Francorchamps, July 1993

The second machine home, eight laps down on the BMW, was a 175 Ducati ridden by Spanish riders Fargas and Rippa. The third team, a further 30 laps in arrears, was another British pair, Peter Inchlay and Robin Good, on a 250 Ariel Sports Arrow. The BMW had taken the lead when Francesco Villa's Ducati broke a valve after 17 hours, just when a

Above
And there are always distractions, like these two young ladies, if one gets bored with the racing

Left
Daffix Eurocol Honda went well in the early stages of the 1993 Spa 24 Hours, but the team was to be sidelined with a blown engine later on

Left

Brian Morrison going for the third victory at Spa – something that was to eventually prove elusive

Above

Yamaha Excusief Team NL lasted until a piston broke after 22.36 hours

repeat of the 1960 result had looked certain.

Ducati were back at Barcelona again in 1962, this time with a prototype Mototrans 250. Piloted by Ricardo Fargas and Enrico Rippa, this machine made a winning debut completing 1,344 miles (591 laps) at an average speed of 56mph, arriving with perfect timing on the finishing line five seconds before the end. Peter Darville and Howard German came second on a 500 Velocette, ten laps behind. Bultaco had their first success in the event, winning the 125cc class.

Montesa, the Barcelona built two-strokes, swept to a one-two-three victory in the 1963 24 Horas. Racing started at 6 pm on Saturday 6 July and during Sunday temperatures topped the 80 mark – almost a welcome relief from the previous day in which Barcelona had been the hottest place in Europe with the thermometer at 92!

It was another triumphant stage in a comeback to motorcycle sport

63

which Montesa were making that year. Winners were the brothers Jorge and Enrico Sirera on a prototype two-fifty version of the 175 Impala Sport, who completed a record 620 laps. Fifth overall and winners of 125cc class were Bultaco, who also claimed fourth spot with one of their newly released 200 Metralla's. The best non-Spanish entry was the British team of Buckmaster/Jackson who finished sixth on a 500 Triumph T100SS, with 555 laps recorded.

If the Montesa victory was impressive, the one scored by Ducati the following year was breathtaking. 1964 not only saw the launch of their legendary 250 Mach 1, but also a record breaking Barcelona 24 Horas victory with a 285cc prototype based on the new 248cc sports roadster, but with its bore increased to 79mm.

By this time, the event's rules allowed factory 'prototypes', although these had, in theory, to be based around a production model. In fact, the

Above
Belgians, Bernard, Feuillien and Fontaine of Pirson Racing ran their Kawasaki KX490 for 409 laps and 24th place at the 1993 Spa marathon.

Right
Night-time at Spa Francorchamps in midsummer is a beautiful sight

Above

*Concentration before the handover.
Veille, however, was to drop the bike
and as a result, the engine was destined
to seize at 11.46 on Sunday*

Right

*CBR600 entered by the Erix-Honda
team at Spa Francorchamps in 1993; 1st
in class and a creditable 18th overall*

winning Ducati, called the Mach 1/S, was far removed from the standard bike and was most definitely a special, expressly constructed for long-distance events.

The riders of this machine were Giuseppe Mandolini and Bruno Spaggiari (who had won for Ducati back in 1957). The pair not only chalked up 635 laps, but also became the first to average more than 100 kilometres an hour (100.293kph). After the finish of the race, Spaggiari made the sign of a cross on the track and vowed he would never race in the Barcelona marathon again.

Special builder Dave Degens created something of a surprise in 1965 by beating the factory teams with his home-brewed 650 Triton (Triumph Bonneville engine, Manx Norton chassis). This was largely the starting point for a succession of specials from the Londoner, thereafter raced under the Dresda label.

On the 9 and 10 July 1966, Montesa won for the fourth time and set a new race record of 646 laps. Another 250 Montesa was second, third a 500 Velocette, fourth a 650 Triumph, fifth a 230 Ossa and sixth another 650 Triumph.

It was Ossa's turn in 1967, when a 230 Sport ridden by Carlos Giro and Luis Yglesias belied its capacity to beat the entire field. In doing so this pairing covered 662 laps, a record which was to stand for several years.

The next highlight in the Montjuich Park classic came in 1970 when Dave Degens returned to score his second victory, this time on a Dresda. British teams took the first four places, headed by 1965 winner Degans and Ian Goddard on Degens' 650 Triumph-engined Dresda. The pair won by 11 laps over veteran Ken Buckmaster and Irishman Austin Kinsella's 650 Triumph. Long-distance experts Peter Darville and Norman Price, whose combined ages totalled 86 years, took a CB750 Honda four into third place after a thrilling tussle with Graham Sanders and Don Jones' 650 BSA twin. Laverda dominated the 1971 event, with their orange 750 overhead cam twins, finishing first, third and fourth, making a very colourful sight.

Bultaco, although by this time concentrating production almost exclusively on off-road motocross and enduro bikes, still found it hard to stay away from tarmac sport and took a renewed interest in the Barcelona race. For the 1972 event, the local factory entered Benjamin Grau and Juan Bordens on the very same 360cc single which had won back in 1969. Classed as a prototype, it employed a modified motocross engine mounted in a road racing frame and sporting an expansion chamber exhaust, twin headlamps, a large capacity tank and a massive 240mm four shoe drum

Finacor Yamaha chased the lead all the way to the flag, but were eventually held to second place by a mere four laps

69

front brake. As in 1969, the combination of two skilled riders and the powerful, light, sweet-handling Bultaco proved unbeatable.

Although they couldn't repeat this success the following year, Bultaco still put in an outstanding performance with the same bike, but different riders. They completed 704 laps, behind the winners Canellas and Grau on the prototype 860cc Ducati v-twin – and ahead of an impressive array of four-cylinder superbikes from the likes of Kawasaki and Honda, to say nothing of works entries from Laverda, Moto Guzzi and BMW.

1974 saw Grau and Canellas back at Montjuich Park, where after 16 hours and with a nine-lap advantage, the Ducati's transmission jammed. However, the winning French team of Godier and Genoud, riding a four cylinder Kawasaki, failed to improve upon Ducati's 1973 record of 1674.58 miles in the 24 hour period.

The following year saw Grau and Canellas improve upon this figure during their winning ride on another Ducati v-twin by an amazing 11 laps, recording 731 laps – 1722.2 miles.

By now the Japanese factories were dominating endurance racing and 1976 saw the leading Ducati down in third spot behind a pair of works Hondas.

Even so Grau, as the factory's main standard bearer, still managed to be 6th in 1978, 3rd in 1979, 2nd in 1981 and 4th in 1982. He also won the event in 1984 after it had been axed from the FIM's official endurance championship. Adding these results to his two wins in 1973 and 1975, he could surely lay claim to the title of outright 'King of Montjuich'. And Ducati themselves were to score another victory in the 24 Horas, when Tejedo and Mallol finished ahead of the field to ensure that the Ducati name was engraved upon the trophy for a record eighth time in 1980.

With the end of the Montjuich marathon in 1986, no rider or factory can ever better these magnificent results of endurance, courage and skill.

American Doug Toland had a second race with the British Phase One equipe. They were to become the first private team to win a 24 hour race for a long time covering 513 laps, 4 laps ahead of Monneret's Yamaha. The win put them both second in the title chase after their fourth in Sweden

Above
Phase One's Steve Manley with his
adrenaline still charging strongly

Right
The successful Phase One trio of (left to
right) Simon Buckmaster, Doug Toland
and Steve Manley enjoying the
celebration of a famous victory

Works support

Endurance racing has made a genuine contribution to the road rider's everyday motorcycle in many areas, such as engine reliability, chassis design and stability at high speed. In this type of long-distance racing – either 1000km, or 6, 8, even 24 hours of sustained rhythm – the effort of reducing mechanical and rider stress to the absolute minimum is of paramount importance. As a result, each team – usually consisting of two or three riders with the technical back-up – attempts to minimize not only the demands on the riders and the machine, but also time involved in pit-stops for repairs and brake and tyre changes.

The atmosphere of a great endurance classic, such as the Bol d'Or or the Le Mans 24 hours, attracts tremendous crowds. Because of this, all the factories (and not just the Japanese) began to involve themselves to an even greater extent beginning in the early 1970s.

Kawasaki were the first of the Oriental manufacturers to realise the contribution endurance racing could exact on its development programme and its publicity department, quickly followed by Honda. Eventually Suzuki and Yamaha followed the same route. European factories too joined in the endurance racing game, with BMW, Ducati and Laverda all entering official teams during the 1970s.

Before the days of Japanese high-finance participation, the endurance racing scene was dominated exclusively by European manufacturers. Bultaco, Montesa and Ossa all made serious challenges. These Spanish factories were gradually replaced by Ducati, Laverda, Moto Guzzi and BMW. Dave Degens with his special Triton and Dresda bikes also came into contention. At Thruxton, Norton won six times and Triumph were victorious with eight victories. But, in truth, time was running out for the production machines, as the first purpose-built endurance racers were to appear in the early 1970s.

One of the most radical of this new breed of endurance racers was the Japauto from Paris.

Japauto's original attempt came in 1969 with a specially prepared CB750 Honda. Accompanied by factory mechanics this bike didn't vary much from the standard roadster. It had twin front discs and a twin-leading shoe

Honda dominated the endurance racing scene for much of the 1970s. Here one of their highly successful RCBs is being put through its paces at Montjuich Park, Barcelona by the British rider Charlie Williams

drum at the rear, de Carbon rear shocks and Dunlop K81 tyres. The welding on the frame was much neater than on the production models, suggesting that the machine was in fact a handbuilt special. The carburettors were stock 24mm Keihins and there was an open four pipe exhaust. Just what was inside the engine neither Honda nor Japauto ever owned up to, but as the gearing was considerably different there was definitely a fair degree of tuning.

The fuel tank carried 28 litres, with fuel consumption averaging 33mpg throughout the machine's winning ride at the 1969 Bol d'Or (which at that time was still held at Montlhéry).

But the really special Japautos didn't arrive until 1972. The reason for this gap was that Honda themselves had tended to stagnate after the 1969 CB750 success (followed by victory in the 1970 Daytona 200 for Dick Mann). Now their engineering staff were kept busy working on cars and on new emission requirements.

The 1972 Japauto not only sported a 950cc big bore Honda RSC (Honda Racing Service) motor, but a Dresda frame, with the whole machine weighing only 170 kg (375 lb).

A year on and Japauto again won the Bol d'Or, this time with a 969cc engine. Official Japanese factory support for endurance racing was now a reality and many of the bikes suddenly became very special indeed, purpose-built for maximum efficiency both on the circuit and in the pits.

Even though they cost much, much more, specialised endurance racing projectiles were rapidly replacing production racers. Modern technology was also on the ascendancy with the appearance of cast alloy wheels, all-round disc brakes, full streamlining, multi-cylinder engines, twin headlamps for maximum night vision, aircraft-type fuel filler caps. Not to mention anything of exotic rear suspension, one-off frames, racing front forks and special factory motors with secret internals.

Ease of access was another consideration, with the increasing use of clips and DZUS fasteners to mount fairings and the like. The effects of crash damage were also taken on board, with components placed in positions where they would be least likely to receive terminal damage in the event of a spill. To speed pit work further, the very minimum of belt sizes was used on a particular bike, reducing the range of tools needed and the confusion likely to be encountered by hard-pressed pit-crew.

This sort of preparation paid dividends, with a much higher level of reliability, even though speeds were rising drastically. But, of course, new problems surfaced, most notably tyre and chain life. Yes, tyres and chains were the big headaches of endurance racing team chiefs of the 1970s. But again improvements in this area were to benefit the normal road rider in future years.

Besides Honda, Kawasaki took an early interest at factory level in

Works support, particularly at the Japanese Suzuka circuit is all about bikes, sales, honour and ... girls, although not expressly in that order

Works support is also about meticulous preparation; no stone is left unturned

endurance racing. This really began in 1974 with Godier and Genoud, who had previously campaigned an Egli-framed Honda. The two G's switched to the new 903cc Kawasaki ZI engine for 1974, with instant success, including victory in the all-important Bol d'Or, where three more Kawasakis followed them home. Again the frame was of Egli design. SIDEMM, the French Kawasaki importer, backed the Godier-Genoud effort, in turn receiving official factory support. The 1975 Bol d'Or – winning Kawasaki of Godier and Genoud had a brand new chassis designed by Pierre Doucque and Michel Lambert. Much effort was expended in improving the machine specially for endurance events. As well as low weight, minimum frontal area, sure-footed handling and instant stopping power, it needed to take into account other important considerations such as ease of maintenance, enough ground clearance, rider comfort and reliability in service.

As the results prove, this theory worked. In the 1975 season, the Godier-Genoud Kawasaki set new records and new standards wherever it appeared. Kawasaki had dominated for two whole years. Honda, of course, now had to respond.

After building a new 750, based on the CB500 four cylinder roadster in 1975 (which proved a dismal failure), Honda retreated back to basics and set up a new research and development department, to replace the old RSC organisation.

RCB's first task was to build a new machine which could not only win events such as the Bol d'Or, but from which a new roadster could be developed. This meant more work, but a much larger research and development budget than would otherwise have been available.

The original RCB engine had a capacity of 941cc, increased to 997 and eventually 999cc. Gear primary drive replaced the usual Honda chain,

Above
The field gets away under the gaze of a packed Suzuka grandstand. The Japanese eight hour race holds the record for the highest attendance of any endurance event

Right
Eddie Lawson came out of retirement for the Suzuka eight hour held on 25 July 1993. Also back was his legendary tuner, Erv Kanemoto. On one of the new RVF (RC45) Hondas, Lawson (together with Satoshi Tsujimoto) came back after a fall to take second place, almost catching the leaders

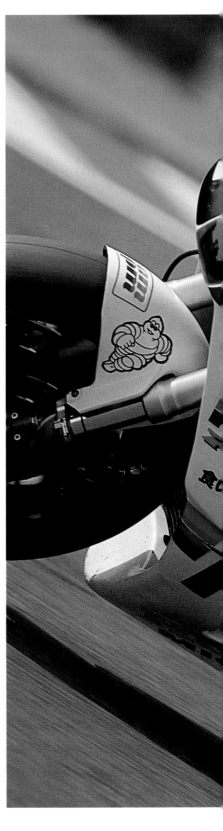

giving the new Honda an unusual whine and providing a convenient countershaft so that the alternator could be mounted atop the gearbox. This effectively reduced engine width to a minimum. Another major change was to the cylinder head which featured not only double overhead camshafts but also four valves per cylinder.

Much time was consumed in arriving at the most effective exhaust system. This needed to be a compromise between noise level, ground clearance and, of course, power output.

The quartet of 32mm Keihin carburettors featured transparent float bowls so an instant check could be carried out for any dirt or other debris within the carburettors themselves.

The ignition system was self-powered using a tiny generator, driven by one of the camshafts, to supply a fully transistorised circuit. After dark

Above
Mick Doohan's Grand Prix commitment meant doing the Suzuka 8 hour with instructions not to come second. He fell, but still managed fourth with partner Daryl Beattie

Right
Takuma Aoki during qualifying for the 1993 Suzuka marathon. With American partner Mike Smith took their 1992 RVF to third with a reliable performance

racing needed powerful lights. These were taken care of by a pair of halogen Cibie units, with a conventional 12 volt battery located in the seat tail.

Although the chassis and suspension were nothing out of the ordinary, a lot of thought had gone into other, less obvious details.

There were many quite noticable innovations scattered around the bike. For a start the wheels were of a new design, with alloy rims and hubs, joined by five sets of spokes (from 1976 Honda fitted steel-spoked Comstar wheels, as later used on a number of their road going models) which were riveted. An experimental 'long-life' drive chain helped cure a potentially weak link, whilst there was eccentric adjustment for the chain located in the swinging arm pivot (from 1977).

The original 941cc motor of 1976 gave 115bhp at 9000rpm. By 1977, with 997cc, Honda could claim 135 bhp and 9500 rpm. A lot of this was thanks to modified carburettors (still of Keihin manufacture) and a new exhaust system. There was also new front and rear suspension, with the rear gas shocks being supplied by Showa; a subsidiary of Honda Motor.

Above

Keiichi Kitagawa and his team-mate Shoichi Tsukamoto took the second full works Kawasaki ZXR-7 to fifth place, sixteen seconds behind Doohan and Beattie

Left

Kitagawa (2) showing excellent form through a chicane at Suzuka

Left

Peter Goddard on the number one factory Suzuki. He later made an error in the dark, slid off and lost himself and Barros three places – dropping them back to seventh

Below

The great Eddie Lawson

Right
While the Grand Prix stars were battling for 1993 Suzuka eight hours honours, Simon Buckmaster and the Phase One team were trying to scrape a few more championship points

Below
The Phase One pit crew in action (Buckmaster seated on bike)

Above

Trick bikes and the latest bits are tested at Suzuka. Pictured here is Hiroyash Tsukiji's 750cc Kawasaki Zephyr, ridden by American Flat Track racers Scott Zampach and Mike Hale in the 1993 event

To ease maintenance, both wheels were now QD, the rear leaving both disc and sprocket left in place. The experimental chain was still being developed, Honda's aim was for it to last a whole 24 hours.

Other less obvious, but still vital, changes were incorporated in the .77 RCB. A reduction of some 20kg was achieved by the use of carbon fibre, mixed with GRP for components such as the fairing, seat and mudguards. The normal lead-celled, acid-filled battery gave way to a smaller, rechargeable, dry-cell assembly. But this particular change was not a success and for 1978 a conventional one was refitted. More weight-saving had come about by attention to minute details, with many small components either hollow or drilled – small savings, but collectively important.

For 1978 Honda came up with another new bike, this time of 999cc capacity. By now the engine was revving to 11,500 and pumped out an

impressive 140bhp. Honda dominated the 1978 endurance season as they had in 1976 and 1977.

Originally the '78 RCB carried its engine lubricant in the frame, but this method only lasted for the first two rounds of that year's Coupe d'Endurance (Zandvoort and Barcelona). Nevertheless Honda still won the series comfortably.

By this time the research and development department had achieved all it had been asked to. Not only were the RCBs virtually unbeatable on the track, but the new Honda roadsters and those in the pipeline had benefited from the endurance race effort.

Amongst these improvements came: longer life drive chains, much superior rear dampers, brighter lights in the shape of quartz-halogen H4 units as standard fitment, Comstar wheels, improved exhausts, whilst later bikes had double overhead camshafts and four valves per cylinder.

Another point worth mentioning was that the '78 RCB bore a closer relationship to roadster practice, with the generator on one end of the crankshaft and the ignition on the other. This had the disadvantage of restricting ground clearance.

After the initial success of the RCB's, Honda Japan organised their endurance racing in a much more comprehensive fashion. There were already several teams from different European countries equipped with RCBs. To bring order to this situation, the Honda Endurance Racing Team was formed. All the countries involved contributed to a central fund, with Honda France taking the leading role.

Four years of involvement had led to a system which was the best ever encountered in this branch of the sport. No wonder other factories could only stare with amazement at what Honda had achieved. Not since the early 1960s had Honda dominated the track in quite the same way. And before this had been a full Grand Prix effort.

Although Honda dominated endurance racing in the mid and late 1970s, other factories were also making an effort during this period.

After Kawasaki, Honda's main challenge came from the Italian Ducati factory. Ducati were able to make best use of the prototype category to develop its line of bevel-driven v-twins. A landmark for them came in July 1973, when Benjamin Grau and Salvador Canellas won the Barcelona 24 hour race on a prototype 860 v-twin. Although the pairing won again in 1975, Ducati could never put together the consistency vital for a serious attempt at the FIM Coupe d'Endurance championship. There were, however, moments of brilliance – the 1000 kilometres at Mugello in 1975, for example, when Canellas was unable to ride, and Grau was partnered

Aoki and Smith change over in the early evening at Suzuka – just study the number of people involved in the pit back-up

by a certain young rider named Virginio Ferrari.

A third place (behind Honda and Kawasaki) was the best Ducati could do in the 1975 championship series. As time went by, it became harder and harder for Ducati (or any other Italian factory) to offer a serious challenge. Only Laverda, with its exotic V-6, was likely to provide real competition. But, sadly, this fascinating project was destined never to fully mature.

Its only appearance on the world stage was at the 1978 Bol d'Or, where after experiencing transmission problems in practice, it was to retire from the race with a failed drive shaft. Ing. Giulio Alfieri, who designed the 2.7 litre V-6 used in the Citroën-Maserati car, was employed as a consultant by Laverda and worked with the company's design chief, Luciano Zen. The machine was constructed over a two year period and made its public debut on the Laverda stand at the 1977 Milan Show, followed by its only competition appearance described above. Riders Cereghini and Perugini retired after some eight and a half hours, but prior to this had been electronically timed at almost 180mph – over 20mph quicker than the winning works Honda RCB999!

So why wasn't this fantastic machine developed to its full potential? Unfortunately the answer is, quite simply, money – or a distinct lack of it. As a result, the failure of the project probably caused the ultimate downfall of this once great Italian marque.

BMW and Moto Guzzi were other European factories who tried, and ultimately failed, to make an impression on the might of the Japanese.

If Honda's all-conquering RCB machines of the 1970s seem impressive, what followed in the next decade would be truly awe-inspiring, with not just Honda, but also Kawasaki, Yamaha and Suzuki all joining in. The era of the full works teams in endurance racing had finally arrived.

Above right
Marc Granie and Yannick Legaudu of France ran their Suzuki (20) in the Superbike category as high as thirtieth place at Suzuka

Right
World Superbike stars Scott Russell (left) and Aaron Slight celebrate their victory in the 1993 Suzuka 8 hours

Opposite
The Japanese rider Kobayaski takes on new tyres; his leathers get over the message.

New technology

Like motocross, endurance racing is all about achieving exactly the right combination of speed, chassis strength, comfort and reliability.

In long-distance racing the fastest engine is of no use whatsoever without equally good brakes, suspension anf frame. At the same time, without reliability and rider comfort, nothing could be achieved either.

A good chassis and suspension is therefore of vital importance; these can take the strain off the rider by making the machine more comfortable and easy to use. They can speed up pit stops by having as many quickly-detachable components combined with the easiest access to parts which require maintenance. They can offer superior protection from the elements and, in the event of an accident, it can even mean less wear to items such as drive chains and tyres.

A pure Grand Prix machine has a very different set of priorities to an endurance bike, and it has to be said that the latter is of far more relevance to the ordinary road rider.

With technology, it was found that what had been good enough to make Honda top dogs in the 1970s was not good enough for the 1980s. Why?

Interesting and technically different Honda powered ELF endurance racer seen at the 1981 Bol d'Or. Commissioned by Honda, it was largely the work of André de Cortanze

ELF with streamlined bodywork; this is the 1982 version. Many of its features were far in advance of its time

The answer is new technology.

Basic motorcycle technology had remained pretty constant for almost eighty years. Of course this didn't mean that there hadn't been developments; in fact there had been very many, all the way from the turn of the century to the end of the 1970s.

But all these features had been developments of the original motorised bicycle concept; as a new piece of technology came along, it was simply traded for what had been there before. Telescopic forks for girders, swinging-arm rear suspension for rigid frames, double overhead camshafts for pushrods, disc brakes for drum brakes, cast alloy wheels for individual spokes and wheel rims – the list is almost endless. Many of these changes had come about thanks to racing and quickly became an accepted part of motorcycling generally.

Apart from the few individuals who tried to change the system – examples being the American Ner-A-Car of the 1920s and the British Difazio-attempts at changing the basic motorcycle concept had been few and far between.

Once again, in the early pioneering days, it was France who took the

lead, in the shape of the radical ELF ('E' for Experimental) endurance racing project.

The first prototype, designed by Andre de Cortanze and powered by a four cylinder Yamaha TZ750 road racing motor, made its track debut at the end of the 1970s. Sponsored by the giant Elf Oil Company, de Cortanze's creation soon attracted attention from Honda, who sent a test rider to evaluate the Yamaha-Elf at a private test session at Le Mans. The result was an agreement with Honda, which was concluded towards the latter half of 1979.

As with the original Yamaha-powered device, the Honda-Elf could loosely be labelled under the heading of hub-centre steering. The general layout of this type of design is as follows: a car-type upright (a light-alloy coasting or forging) supporting either a fixed stub axle or a live rotating axle for one-sided wheel mounting with the brake calipers bolted to the upright. Two one-sided longitudinal arms connect the upright to the main chassis via spherical ball joints. For unbiased steering (effected by a single drag link), the centre of these joints must obviously lie in the centre plane of the wheel. A wide variety of steering geometrics is possible.

In the De Cortanze Yamaha Elf design, there was a fairly conventional steering geometry with some positive offset between the steering axis and wheel spindle. Combined with a conventional rate angle, this achieved the desired trail.

However, the later Honda-engined design employed little offset, with a rake angle of approximately 23 degrees, making steering that much

heavier, but stability that much greater.

De Cortanze had four aims in creating the Elf: to lower the centre of gravity, incorporate 'natural' anti-dive suspension, reduce weight and eliminate the frame completely. There were a number of secondary objectives too, including a 50/50 weight distribution, lower the frontal aspect and reduce the drag factor, change the wheels quickly, simplify chain adjustment and rethink design of the swinging arm are just some of them.

The arrangement with Honda provided de Cortanze with a supply of engines suitable for endurance racing, leaving him free to take care of the cycle parts. The completed Honda-Elf prototype made its debut at the 1980 Bol d'Or, but didn't actually race; this being reserved for the same event the following year.

Ridden by Christian Leliard and Walter Villa the Elf led for the first two laps and stayed in the top six until the rear axle snapped after 8 hours. A replacement was soon fitted, but this would also break later on, sidelining the team.

Following more hard work and many hours out on the test-track a full-

One of the factory-entered Suzuki GSXR750s which had struck troubles out on the circuit in the 1985 Bol d'Or. The GSXR was largely the creation of Yasunobo Fujii, Suzuki's head of European engine development

The GSXR featured a 749cc (70 x 48.7mm) 16-valve double overhead camshaft four-cylinder engine which ran a compression ratio of almost 11:1 in standard form, with a bank of four flat-slide Mikuni carburettors

scale onslaught in the 1982 World Endurance title was planned.

In the end the elf team retired more times than they finished that year, but there were signs that the basic layout was correct. For example, at the Bol d'Or, they qualified 6th fastest in practice, with the Honda-Elf being timed at over 176mph; no other bike 170mph along the Mistral straight. In the race the engine expired after only 4 laps.

Later an NS500 two-stroke Grand Prix motor was built into another Elf chassis, this time to be ridden in the Grands Prix during the mid 1980s by the British rider Ron Haslam. But it was the Elf's appearance in the world of endurance racing which really created the interest. By 1983, the Italian factory Bimota had constructed their own central hub steering bike, the Tesi and the Yamaha GTS1000 touring motorcycle was to come much later.

What of Honda? Well, one feature which was translated in both racing and production models was the Elf single-sided swinging-arm. This consisted of a substantial forged magnesium alloy (or steel on the first Elf endurance models) single-sided swinging-arm which pivoted coaxially with the gearbox sprocket for constant chain tension, and ran on roller bearings.

By the time Honda put this into production (on machines such as the NC40 and RC30 and NSR250R racer), the single-shock with its remote reservoir had been moved from its original position of sitting inboard of the rider's right foot. It no longer worked off the swinging-arm via a set of dural rocker arms with the whole lot attached to the rear of the gearbox via more dural plates, but from a much neater arrangement with the shock mounted centrally within the curved swinging-arm body and a totally revised system of location. As time goes by maybe Honda will make further use of Elf technology in other areas of motorcycle design. Whilst the Honda-Elf project was in its infancy, rivals Kawasaki were making up for lost time. The FIM had introduced the World Endurance Championship in 1980 which had been won by Honda. But all this was set to change with Kawasaki, in association with Serge Rosset, boss of the French Performance company, dominating the series in 1981 and 1982.

The two vast Performance trucks soon became a focal point of the endurance paddock. Containing sufficient facilities to feed and sleep 20 people as well as a superbly equipped workshop, Rosset's team transporters were a visual sign of his total commitment to victory. With additional sponsorship from KVAS oil and KOOL cigarettes, absolutely no effort (or expense!) was spared in building up what was, even by Grand Prix standards, one of the most professional and well structured teams seen anywhere in the world of motorsport.

In contrast to the Honda-Elf avant-garde approach, the Kawasaki-Performance machines were almost conventional in their structure and appearance. The Performance-designed chassis for the endurance Kawasakis was constructed from chrome-moly tubing, bronze welded, with a cast alloy, substantially ribbed swinging-arm for the Uni-Trak rising-rate rocker-arm ATZ single shock rear suspension.

At the front a pair of 40mm Kyaba forks of similar construction to the type used on Korky Ballington's KR500 GP bike, ran in tapered roller

Above right
During the 1980s Honda, Kawasaki and Yamaha all introduced watercooling on their large capacity four-strokes but Suzuki stuck to a mixture of oil and air to achieve its engine cooling. However, by the end of the decade Suzuki finally decided to make the switch to water cooling. Its first production model; the GSXR750WN going into production in the 1992 model year

Right
Rider protection is another area which has seen much change. Not only have helmets become lighter and stronger, but leathers, boots and gloves have also benefited from superior design and materials making them not only more comfortable, but affording increased protection

Yamaha's 'ace-in-the-hole' was the FZ750. Introduced to the public in 1985, the FZ project had begun way back in 1977. Its dominating features were five-valves per cylinder and the radical 45 degree slant of the cylinders

head bearings. A mechanical anti-drive system (again from the KR500) first seen on a BMW Superbike built in the USA in 1976 by Udo Geitl and Todd Schuster, worked by relaying the braking force from the twin 350mm front discs, via a system of pivots and rods, to the fork crowns. It was an effective, although slightly heavier, way of achieving front anti-dive than the hydraulic valving systems used by the other Japanese manufacturers.

Although 18 inch wheels front and rear were occasionally used, mostly a 16 inch (Campagnolo) and 18 inch (Dymag) were standardised. Dunlop tyres were used throughout by the Rosset team, providing excellent grip and wear properties – both of which are vital in endurance racing. Chain adjustment was taken care of by eccentric blocks in the rear of the swinging-arm and integral with the axle.

With the rules stating that engines must be based around the TT Formula 1 – using production-based four-strokes up, 1000cc, or 600cc two-strokes with external engine cases unmodified in any way, the engine chosen was built around the K1000J roadster unit. This air-cooled, across-the-frame-four was specially tuned by Performance. They fitted their own

Left

After the FZ came the FZR (produced in both 750 and 1000 engine sizes with 5-valves or 400 and 600 with 4-valves). One of the early development machines is seen here taking part in the 1987 Bol d'Or

Below

Another area of technology which affects overall performance in racing is tyres. For major events (such as the World Endurance Championship) riders are able to use slicks (shown here), intermediates and wets

Right

V-four technology from Honda, photographed in 1987; the gear driven RVF was developed with endurance racing very much in mind

design of camshafts to the 69.4 x 66mm, 2-valves per cylinder motor, paying particular attention to gas-flowing and porting of the head. The ports were opened out and oversize valves fitted, with twin-plug ignition and 34mm smoothbore Mikuni carbs.

The crankshaft was welded up for extra stiffness, whilst the generator was moved from its normal end of crank location to a position atop the gearbox. Driven by a toothed rubber belt, it charged the battery which was placed just in front of the rear wheel, beneath the rear shock. All this meant that the width of the motor was decreased, giving improved ground clearance; once again an endurance racing modification which would be incorporated by a new generation of roadsters which Kawasaki had in the pipeline.

Running on a compression ratio of 10.8:1, the Performance Kawasaki reliably put out 135bhp at 10000rpm. The six-bearing crankshaft, using roller big-ends and plain small-ends proved more than capable of lasting the full 24 hours and beyond without a hint of trouble.

There was a choice of three possible alternatives for the 2nd and 3rd gears in the 5-speed transmission, depending on exact circuit and rider requirements.

Besides Kawasaki, Suzuki also mounted a challenge to Honda's dominance. Not only had they won the 1980 Bol d'Or (for the very first time) but also another two rounds of the new Endurance World Championship. In January 1981, reports of Suzuki's new endurance challenger began to filter through. The 997cc dohc four-stroke was reputed

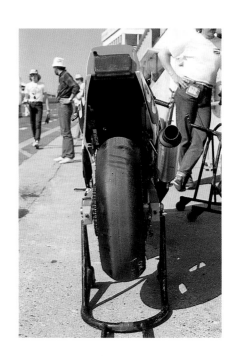

to have bettered 175mph on Suzuki's own test track. The bike featured an interesting rear suspension system with a moto cross style swinging-arm. But just prior to this the former four-time European endurance champion Christian Leon was killed at Suzuka's Japanese test track in November 1980. Tragically, only the day before, he and his former Honda team-mate Herve Moineau had left Honda and signed 1981 Suzuki endurance contracts.

Even though they had lost one of their new signings Suzuki still continued, and although Kawasaki won in 1981 and 1982, Suzuki came good with a vengeance in 1983.

The machine which won the 1983 World Endurance Championship was actually the prototype of what was to emerge as the GSXR750 at the Cologne Show in September 1984.

Right from the start the GSXR was built as a racer first, roadster second. The man who stamped his identity on the project, Yasunobo Fujii, saw to this. His vision was a bike which could not only achieve a genuine 150 mph in standard road-going form, but also become an out-and-out racer with the fitment of a factory race kit developed in conjunction with 'Pops' Yoshimura.

The kit comprised a mouth-watering array of performance goodies including: a gas flowed head, high compression pistons, titanium valve springs, polished carburettor bellmouths, a dry clutch conversion, polished connecting rods, high lift cams and a four-into-one exhaust system.

Yasunobo Fujii was Suzuki's head of European engine development and as such he was one of the team that had led Suzuki into the four-stroke market with the launch of the highly acclaimed GS750 roadster in the late 1970s.

One of the outstanding features of Suzuki's 1983 championship winning endurance racer (and the subsequent GSXR roadster) was its use of oil-cooling; this was new in terms of motorcycle design, but had been used to help control the temperature of aero-engines since at least the early 1920s.

Suzuki first successfully experimented with the idea of curing overheating problems encountered during the development of the XN85 Turbo. Oil jets directed at the underside of the piston crowns prevented the turbocharged engine dropping a molten cocktail into the crankcase. The same idea was also employed on the 1983 GSX750EF motor to prevent the pistons in the two central cylinders running hotter than their counterparts inside.

While it would be accurate to describe the GSX motor as air-cooled with oil assistance, the emphasis was switched the other way in the 'R' engine.

Oil-cooling came into its own in the new system which employed a second oil pump to concentrate on flushing away excess engine heat. A sister unit mounted on the same shaft and sharing a common housing

Right
Part of the Michelin tyre store at the 1993 Bol d"Or. This French company has always been involved with endurance racing

Below right
The Dunlop team with its tyre fitters working hard. Note the cut slick (intermediate) tyre awaiting preparation to the right of the picture. Although now owned by SP Tyres, the famous company is still based at Fort Dunlop, Birmingham, England

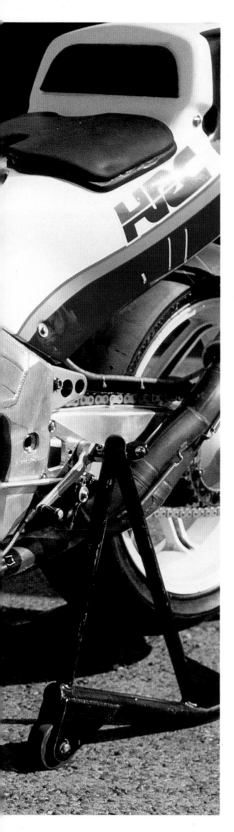

handled the lubrication. Each pump picked up from the sump and pushed oil through the engine at a rate of 20/22 litres per minute.

The flow rate was in fact very similar to that of a conventionally-lubricated engine, but the doubling up of pumps meant a doubling of the circulation. The 5.5 litres of oil carried in the system was passed through a large cooler mounted on the front frame tubes.

Heat dissipation was further aided by the use of a magnesium cylinder head cover and a mass of shallow cylinder head fins which gave the motor a distinctive appearance. All very clever, but why had Suzuki turned to oil cooling in favour of a water jacket?

The answer, claimed Suzuki, was to be found with a measuring tape and a pair of scales. The GSXR was both more compact and a lot lighter than would otherwise have been possible. A prototype using water-cooling was found to be appreciably wider and some 5kg heavier than the oil-cooled engine assembly, which weighed in at just 75kg.

The search for power had led Fujii and his fellow technical staff members down a more conventional path, with improvements to breathing and combustion coupled with moves to reduce frictional losses in the power chain.

The 749cc (70 x 48.7mm) 16-valve double overhead camshaft four-cylinder engine had been subjected to close attention with regard to reducing piston and con-rod weights, without affecting their strength. This had allowed the crankshaft journals to also be reduced in width, compared to the old air-cooled 750EF motor.

The new materials were used for the crankshaft bearings to reduce frictional losses in the transfer of power through the hydraulic clutch and six-speed gearbox.

If oil-cooling was the dominant feature of the GSXR motor, the cycle parts were dominated by the chassis. Fashioned entirely from case and extruded aluminium, the box section full cradle frame also incorporated a light alloy swinging arm and improved 'Full Floater' monoshock rear suspension. At the time the Suzuki publicity people made a big song and dance of the fact that this was the world's first production bike with an alloy frame. Of course 'world's first' is a dangerous claim, and in Suzuki's case they had, in fact, been beaten to this distinction some fifty years before by the German Ardie marque which sold machines with alloy frames back in the early 1930s – even if the technology was somewhat different and the shape vastly more so.

Another 1987 Bol d'Or shot, this time of the oval-piston NR750 machine. Developed from the largely unsuccessful NR500 Grand Prix racer, the NR750 was tested in the hot bed of endurance racing – before it was sold as an exclusive (and extremely expensive) sports roadster

Interestingly, the GSXR endurance racer and its roadster offspring featured an 18 inch front wheel despite the factory having previously convinced everyone and his dog to adopt 16 inches in the interests of ultra-quick steering.

What of the final member of the Japanese 'Big Four', Yamaha? The company had long been a dominant force in Grand Prix and short circuit racing. But in a sport which is very much the preserve of four-strokes, Yamaha with their two-strokes had too often played the hand of the joker on the endurance scene. In 1978, for example, a specially prepared Sonauto OW31 (a 750 four cylinder two-stroke), caused a great deal of excitement in the Bol d'Or, and nearly led to the greatest upset of all time. Ridden by Pons and Sarron, the OW31 not unexpectedly set the fastest practice time, but for the four-strokes, worse was to come. Despite the fact that the bike had to stop more frequently than any other for fuel, it stayed in the lead for nearly 18 hours before its very special crankshaft finally cried enough.

In 1981, Yamaha finally accepted the inevitable and ceased campaigning the two-stroke cause with its Sonauto team of TZ750s, after spending a rumoured £5 million vainly trying to beat the four-stroke.

Sonauto unveiled their own four-stroke challenger in the autumn of 1980, based on the then current XS1100 with a chain final drive conversion. An extaordinary feature of this machine was the girder-style forks, supporting the front end, working on the rocker arm principle, while the rear wheel was mounted in a cantilever system of extremely thin wall tubing – especially unusual when one considers that these engines had a power output bumped up to 120bhp at 9000rpm. But all this effort was a total disaster – there wasn't a single Yamaha-powered machine in the first ten finishers of any of the 1981 season's eight rounds counting towards the Endurance Championship!

This state of affairs was fairly accurately reflected in its showroom sales (at least of large capacity four-strokes) during the same period, with a truly awful range of models highlighted by major flops such as the horrible hi-tech XZ550 v-twin and the ugly XJ650 Turbo.

But to give Yamaha credit it was trying to do something to rescue the situation and produced what would finally emerge as the 'Bike of the Year' in 1985, the FZ750.

In fact, Yamaha were working on the FZ project way back in 1977. What they were looking for was a four-stroke that could equal the power output of two-strokes. Not unnaturally this meant some fairly radical thinking in the engineering department.

A production NR750 being demonstrated prior to the start of the 1993 8 hour race over the Suzuka circuit

Eventually Yamaha was to select a 5-valve per cylinder option, but if anyone thinks this was a little over the top then consider the fact that Yamaha engineers determined that seven valves was the optimum number for getting the highest volume of intake mixture into a combustion chamber up to a rev ceiling of 20,000rpm.

Yamaha even constructed prototype single and four-cylinder engines to test their theories, but came to the conclusion that there were problems with the technology of the day, particularly when it came to putting these ideas into actual production. Yamaha also believed that the 7-valve layout wasn't really suited to the comparatively small displacement engines used in motorcycles. Six valves were tried next but suffered a major problem from hot spots between the exhaust valves. So how about five valves? This proved to be the perfect answer; with two exhaust valves there was enough distance between the pair to eliminate hot spots and the three intake ones still allowed a high inlet volume.

As always with this type of radical engineering, no single component made the FZ into the superb engine it was. The 5-valve layout meant that enough fuel could flow into the combustion chamber to give the potential for class-leading output. The next problem was to burn the stuff efficiently. The 5-valve layout allowed Yamaha to employ a theoretically superior, lens-shaped combustion chamber. Using a single plug, as opposed to the twin plugs used on the experimental 7-valve head, the biconvex chamber gave excellent flame propagation. This then allowed high compression ratios with a slightly dished-topped piston. Overall, this set-up provided a 10 per cent power advantage over a 4-valve head using the traditional pentroof chamber.

In 1982, Yamaha decided that this was the way to go and initiated a variety of project teams all using the 5-valve lens-shaped combustion chamber and a capacity of 750cc to fit in with the upcoming regulations for endurance (and F1) racing. All types of configurations were tried, along with such trickery as hydraulic valve-lifters. No project team was aware of what the other was up to, and when the time came to make the choice, the good old across-the-frame four got the vote.

Even though the basic layout was conventional, there was a radical 45 degree slant of the cylinders which lowered the centre of gravity and enabled Yamaha to employ some of the lessons learnt from looking at current thinking taking place in the four-wheel racing world.

This meant downdraught carburettors with flat slides and inlet tracks to the valves which were straight and of equal lengths. Similarly, the exhaust ports and exhaust header pipes were straighter than would have been possible with an upright engine, or for that matter a V-4.

The generator was positioned atop the gearbox and, not content with the width saving, Yamaha moved the electronic ignition trigger onto the

As Suzuka is owned by Honda it is therefore small wonder that the company display their latest wares and achievements in front of the huge crowds. This is a 1993 view of the machine Honda hoped would be the bike to beat in 1994, the RC45

nearside crank web and mounted the sensors on crankcase halves. The result was that the FZ's crankcases were actually 9mm narrower than the company's XJ400. The width across the barrels was kept down by a hybrid wet/dry liner system which directly water-cooled the top section of the liners only.

The only truly conservative piece of engineering was the central camchain, which Yamaha claimed would have caused unacceptable torque loadings in race trim. But if this statement didn't impress too many people, there were many who applauded the valve train design. There was a cam lobe for every valve – direct operation without rockers – and hollow chrome molybdenum camshafts. Valve lash adjustment was another 'approved' area, with shims under the valve buckets. Yamaha also found a cure for the regular need for valve adjustment. Taking a leaf out of the car designer's brief, they managed to do away with the sort of regular gap adjustment which generations of motorcyclists had come to accept.

The balance of the motor was almost ordinary compared to the top end. There was a 6-speed gearbox and a hydraulic clutch, but other than that it was all standard UJM (Universal Japanese Motorcycle) engineering with a few little dodges like the positive oil-feed to the gearbox, pressure equalizing holes inside the crankcases to cut down on pumping losses, and baffles in the sump to reduce the oil's tendency to slow the crankshaft. All small details, but, again, ones which in total made a significant difference.

Beside that lot the FZ's chassis looked almost ordinary; a box-section job, but made of steel, not alloy, and derived from the YZR500 GP racer. The box-section swinging arm was aluminium alloy, with the rising rate Monocross system. Later in the decade the FZ became the FZR (OWO1 in 750 form) before eventually being superseded by the current YZF.

The 1980s belonged very much to the Japanese, from both technological and endurance racing standpoints, the two often going together. Benchmark bikes like the FZ (and FZR) from Yamaha, the GSXR from Suzuki, together with the Kawasaki GPZ and the Honda's oval piston NR and v-four RVF were all conceived in that decade and their heirs look like being with us well into the future.

Atmosphere

Success in the world of endurance racing can only come with the combination of a fast, reliable, easy handling, comfortable bike with fast, reliable riders and perhaps most of all a dedicated and organised back-up team with cash; lots of it.

To get the real feel (read atmosphere!) of long-distance racing you have to be there. Simply reading race reports in the press, or even watching the event on the television screen is not the same at all.

Russell Benney, the team manager of Phase One (British endurance team which won the 1993 Spa 24 hours), sums up endurance racing thus 'It's a drug, totally intoxicating', and in the same breath continues 'It knackers you, wrecks your body, eats your time, money and social life.' Russell should know; not only is he the driving force behind Phase One, he has been closely involved with endurance racing ever since he began on a Harris-framed Kawasaki at the Bol d'Or in 1985. Since then he's done every European round and raced on FZ750, RC30 and ZXR750, before finally retiring from the saddle and becoming team manager.

Besides the rider and the manager, there are all the unsung heroes of endurance; the coffee makers, the wives, the girlfriends and sponsors, not to say anything of the team of dedicated mechanics. No other branch of motorcycle sport demands quite so much from so many bodies. And 'team' is the operative word; all have to pull in the same direction, otherwise there are major problems.

Long-distance racing reached something of a zenith during the mid/late 1970s. This coincided with a boom in motorcycling generally and organisers of events such as the Bol d'Or and the Le Mans 24 hour, were able to exploit this situation not only to their own financial advantage, but for the furtherance of the sport too.

Although endurance races were staged in other countries, it was the French who led the way. Realising that a long race won't hold the attention of spectators for its complete duration, side shows were laid on, making the events cover much wider interests – almost becoming festivals – particularly the Bol d'Or.

At its new location over the Paul Ricard circuit in the south of France,

Endurance racing has its own special breed of excitement, glamour and colour. All three virtues are expressed in the excellent all-action shot by photographer Mark Wernham of Monneret's Finacor Yamaha at the Bol d'Or classic in September 1993

Left

Another facet of the endurance scene is the sideshows; typical is this 'big-wheel' from Suzuka 1993

Above

This type of 'burn-out' entertainment in front of the vast Le Mans stand helps to keep the crowds flocking to endurance events – even when, in 1989, Le Mans lost its official World Championship status and became, temporarily, the FIM Cup

the event benefited from the much improved weather, a change from the the colder, duller skies usually seen at the more northerly Le Mans track.

Paul Ricard is a purpose-built course and the visitor is well catered for with a vast array of amenities including an off-road training ground, airship, superb on site facilities and of course the circuit itself which offers excellent spectator visibility, with banked areas or grandstands dotted all around the 3.549 mile track. Rider safety is also good, with run-off areas and safety fences on corners. Closed-circuit television monitors keep everyone in touch with the racing, latest results and interviews.

As well as permanent bars and restaurants within the circuit, many other stalls sell a wide variety of food and goods. There is even a kiddies' funfair, karting circuit and various support races during the four days or so over which the Bol d'Or lasts.

Besides France, the 'home' of endurance racing, other countries have

Left
Taking race detail to the crowd, on huge screens around the circuit is a feature of the Suzuka eight hours

Above
A lovely woman with a pit board adds a touch of glamour to the night-time hours at Spa, July 1993

Above right
Typical privateer pit bay, Anderstorp June 1993. Colourful although not particularly busy at this stage

Right
With a successful rider changeover just completed, getting back into the foray is the immediate priority

Left
Factory Honda pit area at the 1987 Bol d'Or. Crowds of people but no panic. Every pit member has his own task

Right
Very confident and cool, Doug Toland with the British Phase One Kawasaki ZXR750. Experience is the key to the success of this private team run by Russell Benney, with several backers, notably Riders of Bridgewater

Below
Bruno Bonhuil in relaxed mood waits to take over the Suzuki at Bol d'Or

contributed, notably Belgium (Spa), Holland (Zolder), Japan (Suzuka), Spain (Barcelona), Britain (Thruxton) and Sweden (Anderstorp). All these events provide their own atmosphere and the Suzuka eight-hour also sets the record for the world's highest attendance for a motorcycle event. The Suzuka meeting also has a record of attracting the world's top stars. For example in 1993, World Superbike contenders Scott Russell and Aaron Slight scored a memorable win for Kawasaki and the Coca Cola sponsored Suzuka 8 hours. The big 'K' men beat the Kanemoto Honda ridden by the multi time 500cc World Champion Eddie Lawson and the Japanese rider Satoshi Tsujimoto.

Mick Doohan and Daryl Beattie had previously qualified the Team HRC RVF Honda on pole. Doohan was leading the race in his second session but crashed, eventually the Honda pair finished fourth.

Just to prove that you don't have to be a works star to win the World Endurance crown, 1993 saw American privateer Doug Toland become champion after all his rivals either fell off or broke down at the final round at Paul Ricard (Bol d'Or).

The Japanese take the Suzuka result very seriously. Trick bikes and new technology are often brought out for the Suzuka 8 hours in an attempt to upstage the opposition. There are also huge screens around the circuit to keep the crowds informed of every aspect of the race. Like the Bol d'Or, Suzuka can boast the very best facilities. Yes, both the French and Japanese know the correct formula.

Present and future

Where is endurance racing going? Will it fail or will it prosper? These are burning questions. When the 1994 calendar appeared it was seen that there would only be four rounds – Le Mans, Spa, Suzuka and Paul Ricard (Bol d'Or). Other rounds in Sweden and Indonesia didn't actually get the green light.

Marathons have suffered before, but they have always survived and come back to be even stronger. Will it happen this time? One cannot be sure, but the signs look promising.

Left

The 1993 Bol d'Or saw the Italian Ducati factory race two works 888s (a third French-entered semi-works model also took part). This was an attempt to repeat the success the marque has scored at World Superbike in recent years

Below

Sadly none of the Ducatis lasted the distance. Their pits often looked very confused, lacking the smoothness of the other works teams. It is hoped that they have learned from this experience and will be back in future years

All motorcycle sport depends upon support from riders, manufacturers and, most of all, spectators. It seems that France and Japan have no problems in these areas, but other countries continue to struggle.

In 1993 there were five rounds – the 1994 list, plus Anderstorp in Sweden. The first to be staged was Le Mans on 17-18 April. There was no lack of potential winners, although Wilfred Veille had to be drafted in to replace Englishman Terry Rymer after the latter had crashed during qualifying. Veille himself was destined to suffer from an old injury which was not fully mended. Eventually the race was won by the team of Veille and Morrison, riding a Kawasaki France ZXR750.

Next came Anderstorp on 18-20 June. The race itself was faced with a lot of complications before it got underway, and when it did the track was treacherously wet. However, as at Le Mans, the damp conditions suited Scotsman Brian Morrison admirably and with team-mates Veille and

Above
Marathon racing is all about finishing. By Sunday morning at the 1993 Bol d'Or Haquin, Ch Artiques and Guilard had succeeded in taking their own private Kawasaki to third place and a rostrum finish

Right
Brian Morrison on a factory Kawasaki was the most fancied runner in the 1993 World Endurance Championship, but his retirement at the Bol d'Or and Toland's sixth place points ensured that the championship was lost

Above

The unfortunate Simon Buckmaster was involved in a horrific accident whilst taking part in the 1993 Bol d'Or

Left

Factory Suzuki rider Jean Marc Deletang taking his Suzuki towards a well-earned victory in the 1993 Bol d'Or

Battistini, they managed to chalk up another win to comfortably lead the championship.

The surprise of this round was the local team of Bosson, Linden and Skold, who used their track knowledge to full effect with a superb second spot on their ageing RC30 Honda. Peter Linden is a pilot in the Swedish Royal Air Force; he was certainly using all his 'flying' experience at Andersdorp.

At the half-way stage was reached in the championship, the teams travelled to the famous Spa Francorchamps circuit set deep in the Ardennes forest in eastern Belgium. By the end of the gruelling marathon, the winner was the British privateer Phase One team of Steve Manley, Simon Buckmaster and American Doug Toland.

The pre-race favourites, Morrison, Veille and Battistini on the works Kawasaki retired with three hours to go, with a blown engine. When it returned the ZXR was in third place some eight laps behind the leaders, and had very little chance of making up the difference.

Very, very few privateer teams win World Endurance Championship races, so this was a truly superb achievement.

Another notable success was the fifth position gained by Eckert, Scherm and Lewign who rode a Honda CBR600 against a hoard of 750s which included YZF and OWO1 Yamahas, GSXR Suzukis, ZXR Kawasakis and various V-four Hondas.

Phase One's Spa victory had only been mirrored twice during the previous decade : in 1984 by Johan van der Wal's Roadrunner Suzuki team at Le Mans, and in 1991, when the French Finacor Yamaha team won at Le Mans.

Phase One rider Steve Manley was speaking for the whole Phase One equipe when he said: 'It's difficult for a privateer (team) to win but we've shown it can be done. We led the race more than anybody else, even the works Kawasaki — I just couldn't believe the atmosphere. I could hear the cheering and see the Union Jacks waving. It was so emotional and really got through to me.'

At Le Mans, in the first round of the 1993 championship, Phase One's new team of Buckmaster, Manley and Mark Linscott was running fourth and looking on for third place when Linscott crashed out. For the Andersdorp 24 hour race, team manager Russell Benney had planned to run Colin Gable in place of Linscott, but Gable injured a hand at the Isle of Man TT and was therefore ruled out. Instead, Doug Toland was drafted in and the team finished an impressive fourth.

As recounted in the previous chapter, Scott Russell and Aaron Slight won the prestigious Japanese Suzuka 8 hour on a full works Kawasaki. However, Eddie Lawson had come out of retirement to rejoin his tuner Erv Kanemoto on one of two new RVF (prototype of RC45) Hondas. After

Left

The remains of Buckmaster's Phase One Kawasaki, he was severely injured and would have been unable to return to the bike if a repair had been possible

Right

Simon Buckmaster had been involved in a collison with the Suzuki factory rider Graziano during the night. Shown here prior to the accident, the Suzuki rider was able to push his machine back to the pits and it was out again one hour later, whilst the Englishman's injuries were so severe as to end his racing career

Below

Big news for the Bol d'Or was the European launch of the Honda RC45

a fall, they came back to runner-up spot, almost catching the leaders in the process. While the Grand Prix stars were battling for eight-hour honours, the Phase One team was attempting to scrape together a few championship points.

And so to the final confrontation at the Bol d'Or, held over the 18-19 September. The Bol d'Or always attracts great attention and massive crowds. 1993 was no exception and there was also to be high drama. First came the European launch of Honda's new RC45. Then Ducati stunned the endurance racing world by turning up with a pair of full works V-twins in addition to the two works Kawasakis and two works Suzukis.

Not only was the appearance of the factory Ducatis a massive boost to the race, but the riders themselves were noteworthy. Amongst them was double World Superbike Champion (1991 and 1992) Doug Polen, who teamed up with factory Ducati rider Stephane Mertens, and Polen's 1993 USA teamster Pascel Piccotte.

Aboard the second Ducati was another former double World Superbike champion Fred Merkel, who was teamed with 250 Grand Prix rider, New Zealander Simon Crafer and Florian Ferracci (whose father owns the Fast by Ferracci team).

Finally there was a semi-works Ducati team consisting of Frenchmen Phillippe Mouchet, Bertrand Sebileau and Crysty Rebuttini.

Seventy riders lined up opposite their bikes and then sprinted across the track and leapt aboard as the clock hit three and the lights turned to green. Amid the deafening roar, Mertens was away first, swiftly followed

RVF-RC 45 **HONDA**
présentation européenne
bol d'or 1993

by Crafer, Mouchet, Moineau, Sarron, Rymer (the 1992 champion) and
Bontempi.

Unbelievably, as the riders came round to complete the first circuit,
Ducatis were in a 1-2-3 position and the crowd went wild with delight. By
lap two, Crafer was in the lead but the Suzukis were beginning to zero in
on the thundering Italian V-twins and soon Moineau was using the
Suzuki's superior top end to blitz past the Bologna missiles and into the
lead.

There was no respite during the first quarter of the race and, with so
many excellent bikes and class riders, the race was running more like a
short circuit event than a twenty-four hour marathon.

Both factory Ducatis lost valuable time in the pits; in fact lack of
organisation from the Italian team was a major embarrassment. However,
Ducati were not alone, as the works Kawasakis suffered from overheating
in the early stages, so both bikes ran on with their fairing lowers removed.
Meanwhile the GSXR Suzuki of Moineau, Graziano and Lavielle led for
the first five hours, but dropped down the table when Graziano was
involved in a collision with Phase One teamster Simon Buckmaster in the
dark at the fast left-hander following the start-finish straight.

Graziano was able to continue after pushing the Suzuki back to the pits,
but the luckless Buckmaster had suffered a serious injury to his left leg
and was flown by helicopter to Marseille hospital for emergency
treatment.

The leading Suzuki's crash allowed Rymer/Morrison/Bonoris (Kawasaki)
to take the lead, with Sarron/Bonhuil/Deletang (Suzuki) second, one lap
adrift. Third was the French semi-works Ducati team of
Mouchet/Sebileau/Rebuttini. The first full factory Ducati was sixth. Some
further sloppy pit-work (and a spate of problems) dropped the Italian
bikes further down the field.

In typical endurance racing fashion anything can happen, and it finally
did around the 18 hour mark. This third quarter of the 1993 Bol d'Or was
marked by a whole clutch of retirements, with four of the six works
machines falling by the wayside.

Brian Morrison's chance of becoming World Endurance Champion
vanished when the engine of his Kawasaki blew apart. His nearest
challenger Wilfred Veille, on the second works Kawasaki, also went out of
the running when his engine suffered a terminal blow-up. All three
Ducatis finally expired: Mertens/Polan/Picotte(clutch),
Crafer/Merkel/Ferracci (engine) and finally the
Mouchet/Sebileau/Rebuttini (broken crankcases) led to a glum set of faces
in the Bologna camp. All these disasters were instrumental in promoting
Dominique Sarron, Jean Marc Deletang and Bruno Bonhuil and their
GSXR Suzuki to the number one spot, a position they were to hold to the

Right
*The works Suzuki mechanics work
frantically to repair Graziano's machine*

Below right
*Left to right B Bonhuil, D Sarron and
JM Deletang receive the Bol d'Or
Trophy after winning the 1993 race*

Below
*Kawasaki France pit stop; but it wasn't
to be glory that year. Both works
Kawasakis retired*

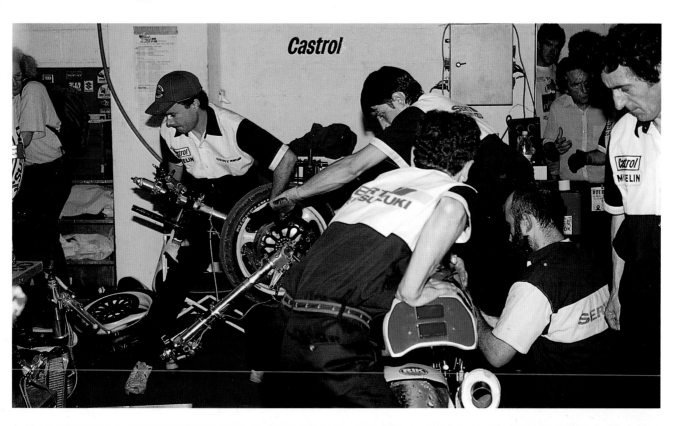

Right

From third place in the morning of the 1993 Bol d'Or the Moto-Sport Courneuven team eased off the pace to save the bike and ensure a top nine finish, giving Doug Toland sufficient points to win the riders' Endurance World Championship title

Below

Doug Toland (yellow leathers) celebrates his new title on the rostrum, a day he will remember for the rest of his life. In what other branch of motorcycle sport could a true privateer beat the world ? It could only happen in endurance racing

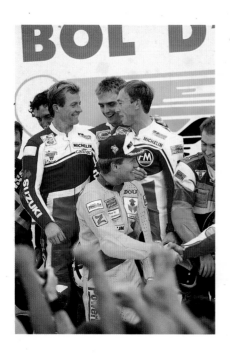

end. The race was actually red-flagged some one hour and five minutes before the scheduled end, due to the customary track invasion by a vast section of the sun-kissed 100,000 crowd.

The riders' and pit crew's enthusiasm was a lot more muted, not only due to the long hours in the saddle and hard work by the spannermen and their helpers, but also by the news that poor Simon Buckmaster had lost the lower part of his leg in the earlier crash, even though doctors had performed two operations involving micro surgery.

This personal tragedy only underlines the real commitment put into endurance racing by the riders. One places confidence in riding ability and machine preparation in any form of motorcycle sport, and none more so than endurance racing, but there are no guaraentees out on the track.

With the European debut of Honda's new RC45 it seems the Japanese giant is about to make a serious return to marathon racing. With continued development by the other Japanese manufacturers, and it seems possibly Ducati, endurance racing appears set to continue to thrill the crowds and fascinate the motorcycle aficionados, even though the number of rounds has been reduced.